CALLED

HOW JESUS TRANSFORMED
ORDINARY PEOPLE
INTO DISCIPLES

© 2022 Lifeway Press®
Reprinted June 2022, Jan. 2023, Apr. 2023, June 2023, Sept. 2023

ISBN 978-1-0877-4912-9
Item 005833726
Dewey Decimal Classification Number: 242
Subject Heading: DEVOTIONAL LITERATURE / BIBLE STUDY AND TEACHING / GOD

Printed in the United States of America

Student Ministry Publishing
Lifeway Resources
200 Powell Place, Suite 100
Brentwood, TN 37027-7514

We believe that the Bible has God for its author; salvation for its end; and truth, without any mixture of error, for its matter and that all Scripture is totally true and trustworthy. To review Lifeway's doctrinal guideline, please visit www.lifeway.com/doctrinalguideline.

Unless otherwise noted, all Scripture quotations are taken from the Christian Standard Bible®, Copyright © 2017 by Holman Bible Publishers. Used by permission. Christian Standard Bible® and CSB® are federally registered trademarks of Holman Bible Publishers.

PUBLISHING TEAM

Director, Student Ministry
Ben Trueblood

Manager, Student Ministry Publishing
John Paul Basham

Editorial Team Leader
Karen Daniel

Writer
Will Cumby

Content Editor
Kyle Wiltshire

Production Editor
Brooke Hill

Cover Design
Kaitlin Redmond

Graphic Designer
Shiloh Stufflebeam

TABLE OF CONTENTS

INTRO

There are seven lanes, each with an anxious sprinter crouched in the launch position, holding a baton. All the sprinters want to do is go. It is the 4 X 100 relay race, and there is a crowd of witnesses waiting, watching, and expecting. The crowd's roar around them is deafening, yet each sprinter's focus only allows them to hear the sound of their pounding heartbeat as they anticipate the explosion from the starter pistol. Go-time is coming. "On your mark" echoes from the speakers. The sprinters back themselves into the starting blocks. It is about to happen. Their hands are correctly positioned on the track markers. "Get set." The sprinters raise their hips. The crowd quiets. POW!

The track is your life and the baton is the gospel—the good news of Jesus. That pounding heartbeat is God's command to share the good news, and the starter pistol firing is the moment when you, in faith, accept Jesus into your life. We all share the command to win others for Jesus. It is what we are all called to do. You are called in your specific context to go and make disciples of your neighbors, your teammates, your classmates, your family, and your community. When one person accepts Jesus, it is a win for all of us. We are called to go and share the good news of Jesus.

Friend, God has called us to go. But before we launch, I want to share some instructions with you. If you don't know where you are going, you will end up somewhere you do not intend to go. We are not running aimlessly or selfishly. There is a track under our feet that we are to run on.

Every story of victory has a standard of success. The standard is someone or something that came before and set the mark to shoot for. For the next 30 days, we will look at our standard—the life of Jesus and how He made disciples. He wants us to go and do the same. Lace up your cleats. Let's head to the track and prepare for the race that is set before us. It's time to answer the call.

GETTING STARTED

This devotional contains 30 days of content, broken down into sections. Each day is divided into three elements—discover, delight, and display—to help you answer core questions related to Scripture.

discover |

This section helps you examine the passage in light of who God is and determine what it says about your identity in relationship to Him. Included here is the daily Scripture reading, focus passage, along with illustrations and commentary to guide you as you explore God's Word.

delight |

In this section, you'll be challenged by questions and activities that help you see how God is alive and active in every detail of His Word and your life. We've given you a whole page to write your answers to these questions, so really think and dig in.

display |

Here's where you take action. Display calls you to apply what you've learned through each day's devotion.

> **Each day also includes a prayer activity at the conclusion of the devotion.**

Throughout the devotional, you'll also find other resources to help you connect with the topic, such as Scripture memory verses, additional resources, and articles that help you go deeper into God's Word.

THE PEOPLE JESUS CALLED

Everyone has a unique story, and no two stories are exactly alike. In section one of this book, we'll explore the different ways Jesus called people to be one of His disciples. As you read their stories and see the differences, you might see a piece of your story there as well. No matter if your calling was loud and exciting or more like a quiet whisper, His message remains the same—follow Me.

LET'S GO!

discover |

READ MATTHEW 28:18-20.

Jesus came near and said to them, "All authority has been given to me in heaven and on earth. Go, therefore, and make disciples of all nations, baptizing them in the name of the Father and of the Son and of the Holy Spirit, teaching them to observe everything I have commanded you. And remember, I am with you always, to the end of the age."

Most people are usually very productive right before they go on vacation. Chores are done, checklists are cleared, and instructions for how to take care of the dog are meticulously detailed for those left in charge. Think about the last time you went somewhere. How focused were you to make sure everything was in order before you left?

In the final verses of Matthew 28, Jesus left specific instructions for His disciples. These were challenging yet straightforward instructions. This next step would require them to fully live what they learned and teach everyone about Jesus regardless of their backgrounds, cultures, or ethnicities. The best part about Jesus's charge to His disciples is that He didn't just leave a note and expect them to share His story by themselves. Jesus had a face-to-face conversation with His disciples then promised to be with them along the way as they made new disciples, baptized, and taught others.

How will your friends know Jesus if you do not share Him with them? Jesus is telling you, like He told His disciples, "Let's go!"

delight

When was the last time you told someone about your faith in Jesus?

How does it make you feel to know that you never have to share your story/God's story alone?

display |

Consider the part of Jesus's story that gives you the most peace, joy, or strength. How can you go and share that part of His story with someone who needs it? Write out a plan below for how you can share the peace, joy, or strength you receive from Jesus with someone else this week.

Dear Jesus, I know You want me to go and that You promise to go with me. I pray that You not only show me someone who can benefit from knowing Your story but also that You would help me to be faithful to share it with them. Amen.

CALLER ID

discover |

READ LUKE 5:1-11.

When Simon Peter saw this, he fell at Jesus's knees and said, "Go away from me, because I'm a sinful man, Lord!" —Luke 5:8

Caller ID is one of the most incredible cell phone features. You can see who is calling before you answer. Although you can refuse the call, you cannot stop someone from placing the call or leaving you a message. Have you ever had one of those days where you were very glad you had caller ID and silenced every call you received?

In this passage, Peter, also known as Simon Peter, and his friends were done fishing after a long unproductive day. They weren't just taking a break, they were finished. Then, Jesus showed up and asked them to push out from shore so He could use their boats as a platform to teach the crowds that gathered. When He was finished teaching, Jesus told Peter to try fishing again. At this point, Peter would have rather silenced Jesus's call, but He didn't. He obeyed and He saw a miracle. At that point, the shame of his past came rushing to the surface.

Friend, your past is a platform, not a prison. Peter tried to disqualify himself, but Jesus took the emptiness of Peter's past and turned it into a platform for God to use. Jesus didn't try to convince Peter that a miracle would happen; He just spoke and offered an opportunity. The door was left open for Peter to decide. When Jesus calls us, we can deny the call, but we can't stop it from taking place. When we respond like Peter did, life-changing miracles can happen to us. Don't silence Jesus's call because of your past. Let it be His platform for God to use.

Called

delight |

How has Jesus used your past as a platform to tell others about Him?

Why do you think Jesus chose someone who called himself sinful to help save others?

display |

Realize that those with the worst past can still have the best future through Jesus. Today, look for an opportunity to share your story with someone about how Jesus turned your past into a platform for His praise. Prepare by writing out your story below. How has Jesus taken your past and turned it into His platform?

God, help me see that my past is a platform, not a prison. Give me the confidence to be a living light that shines in such a way that when I share my story, others are convinced by Your goodness and love to walk out of their dark spaces also. Amen.

DAY 3

WILLING TO GO

discover |

READ MATTHEW 4:21-22.

Going on from there, he saw two other brothers, James the son of Zebedee, and his brother John. They were in a boat with Zebedee their father, preparing their nets, and he called them. Immediately they left the boat and their father and followed him.

Yesterday, we learned about a fisherman who was washing his nets, which symbolized he was done fishing. Today, we meet two more fishermen, except this time they were preparing their nets to begin fishing. In other translations of the Bible, the word "mending" is used, implying the brothers were repairing broken nets.

At some point, these nets worked, but certain circumstances caused them to become worn. We also see that these fishermen were not alone. They were brothers working together with their father. How often have you looked at what you have and thought, "If only I had better stuff, I could do more"? These brothers may have felt the same way on the day Jesus walked by.

When Jesus walked their way, He made a simple request: "Follow me." At that moment, two brothers working on their nets were moved to go. Jesus called James and John—simple fishermen—but they willingly walked away from their nets and father to follow Him. When we connect to something greater than ourselves, it will increase our authority, ability, and activity. God can use ordinary people like you and me who understand that He is extraordinary and can do mighty things through them. We just have to be willing to go.

delight |

Why do you think Jesus called ordinary people like James and John?

How does connecting to something greater than yourself enable you to do more than you could do alone?

display |

You are greater because of the greatness that lives in you—the Holy Spirit. I challenge you to see the ordinary things about you or things you like to do as extraordinary because God can use them. I also encourage you to be like Jesus and see people who feel ordinary and help them see how extraordinary they are through a relationship with Christ. We don't have to put on new clothes or a new face to follow Jesus. We just need to be willing to go!

Write a list below of traits or qualities about yourself that may seem ordinary. Next to it, write out ways that God has or can do extraordinary things with these ordinary abilities.

Ordinary	Extraordinary

Today, God, we recognize how super You are and how our connection to You takes our natural being and helps us do the supernatural. Help us also to see possibility in others and encourage them to know You more. Amen.

MY PHONE IS DRY?

discover |

READ MATTHEW 9:9-13.

As Jesus went on from there, he saw a man named Matthew sitting at the tax office, and he said to him, "Follow me," and he got up and followed him. —Matthew 9:9

One of the most challenging parts of school can be figuring out who your people are. It can be hard to know which lunch table to sit at or which crowd to hang with in the courtyard. The wrong crowd could get you labeled for the entire school year. Unfortunately, people can be very mean. Individuals will cut someone off just because they don't agree with some aspect of their life. Thank God we have the opportunity to belong to a crew that universally accepts us despite our skin colors, our neighborhoods, popularity levels, or our pasts.

I like that when Jesus walked by, Matthew was working. Jesus saw Matthew and also saw what he was doing. Tax collectors were not popular because many were sneaky. Jesus knew that even an unpopular man who was probably stealing money from others deserved the chance to change.

Have you heard the phrase, "My phone is dry"? That means you are not getting any calls, texts, or other forms of communication, and you have nothing to do. When your phone is dry, you're more likely to take a call from anyone and go almost anywhere. If Matthew had a phone, I bet that one call to go would have shaken him out of his seat. God called you—just like Matthew—despite your popularity or past and wants you to join Him in His mission. One call from someone special can change anyone. You don't have to be popular and loved by all to be a disciple of Jesus.

Called

delight |

How does it feel to receive a call from someone special when you feel like no one is calling?

Why do you think Jesus called Matthew while Matthew was working in an unpopular profession?

display |

People are picked on because they stand out or are different from others. Jesus picked you because you stand out to Him, and He wants you to select others to stand for Christ. Talk to the person that God has highlighted in your life. Genuinely listen to their story, then ask God to help you encourage them. Write their name below and ask God to help you cross paths with them today.

God, we thank You that You can call us even when we feel no one wants to speak to us, and You can call us away from lifestyles that are against Your will for our lives. Help us to see others who feel unseen, unpopular, and unwanted. Encourage us to share Your love for them and Your acceptance of everyone. Amen.

143

discover |

READ JOHN 3:1-21.

"How can anyone be born when he is old?" Nicodemus asked him. "Can he enter his mother's womb a second time and be born?" —John 3:4

One of the coolest things about technology is that it's always advancing and getting better. Not that long ago, the primary way to contact people was through mailing a physical letter. When I was in high school, people carried beepers or pagers. If you wanted to reach someone, you had to find a phone connected to a wall plug, call the pager number, then type in a call back number or code that meant something. One of the most popular pager codes was "143," which means I love you. If you want to say I love you today, there are cell phones, social media accounts, email, internet apps, and many more ways to do it.

Jesus simply called Peter and the other disciples, but He had to use a different technique to capture Nicodemus's heart and convince him to become a disciple. Nicodemus didn't understand when Jesus spoke about being "born again," but we know that at some point along the way the light bulb came on. Check out John 19:38-42. When Jesus died on the cross, Nicodemus was one of the people who took care of His body and helped Him into His (temporary) tomb.

Today, I want you to see that God knows just how to reach those He is calling to Himself. Just like with Nicodemus, God will use the best form of communication to get people's attention and tell them 143— "I love you."

delight |

What are the different ways God gets people's attention?

Why do you think God uses multiple methods to call people to follow Him?

How did God get your attention?

display |

God wants us to go tell people about Him, and there are many ways to share the story of Jesus. Take a few minutes today and come up with three ways to share your faith beyond physically talking to someone.

 1.

 2.

3.

God, we thank You that You can creatively call those who need to know You. Help me to discover inventive ways that I can share the gospel with my friends, my family, and my community. Amen.

IDENTITY

discover |

READ MARK 10:17-22.

Looking at him, Jesus loved him and said to him, "You lack one thing: Go, sell all you have and give to the poor, and you will have treasure in heaven. Then come, follow me." —Mark 10:21

When someone is asked about their identity, they often refer to what they own or something they do or participate in. The truth is, your identity is more about who you belong to than what you possess or are good at. You are not just an athlete—that is what you do. You are more than a student at a certain school—you are a co-heir with Jesus to God's kingdom.

In today's passage, we find a guy who seemingly had it all. He was rich, young, and in charge! He definitely would have had a blue check on his Instagram account. This guy was knowledgeable about Jesus and the law, but we quickly find out he didn't fully know Jesus. Jesus challenged the young ruler with a question without raising His voice or being rude. The rich young ruler was shocked. He was looking for what he could do to have eternal life within the borders of his own abilities. When Jesus challenged him to part with his possessions, the man's excitement turned to sadness.

Friend, we do not have to do anything to receive God's grace, and God does not require any less than what He has given us. God will also give us a gentle nudge when He sees our priorities are out of place. You are God's wonderful creation, and He wants your whole heart more than your things.

delight |

Why do you think the Bible mentioned Jesus loving the man before He challenged him?

How do you think the man would have felt if Jesus only asked him to sell some of his possessions? What mattered most to Jesus?

What is something you could let go of to have more room for Jesus?

display |

Jesus has different ways of pointing out areas that we need to address. Take a look at your priorities and God's position in your life. Do you label yourself by what you own or what you do before you claim Christ? Jesus was not rude when He challenged the rich young ruler, and He is not rude about challenging you. Accept the challenge and choose Christ. When you encourage your friends to position God above possessions, consider your tone and do everything in love.

God, we thank You for Your grace. Help us see spaces where we have chosen our possessions or even our position over You. We apologize when we are guilty of doing this. As we tell others about You, help us encourage our friends to also choose You first with love. Amen.

Memory Verse

MATTHEW 28:18-20

Jesus came near and said to them, "All authority has been given to me in heaven and on earth. Go, therefore, and make disciples of all nations, baptizing them in the name of the Father and of the Son and of the Holy Spirit, teaching them to observe everything I have commanded you. And remember, I am with you always, to the end of the age."

LIVING WATER

discover |

READ JOHN 4:1-26,39-42.

Jesus answered, "If you knew the gift of God, and who is saying to you, 'Give me a drink,' you would ask him, and he would give you living water." —John 4:10

One of the things I love most about the Bible is how it remains relevant. In addition to that, every time I read it, I discover something new. Jesus is for everyone, and anyone who chooses to accept Him will find a fresh perspective and a joy to tell others about Him.

Today's story explores a Samaritan woman who met Jesus at a well. Here's the thing: Jesus didn't need to go through Samaria. He could have gone another way. Jews were not supposed to be friendly with Samaritans, and women did not draw water from the well at noon nor by themselves. Thank God, Jesus didn't allow social conventions or racism to interfere with His desire to make disciples. Jesus met this woman at the well in her private world, shared His love, and she became a proud disciple of Jesus.

God will step over every roadblock to build relationships and build His kingdom. The passage says that Jesus's water is living, like a fresh, bubbling spring. That means God's Word and God's love are not stagnant. They stay fresh. The same Jesus that creatively reached a woman who had every obstacle to block her from knowing Him will inevitably break down every barrier and reach every generation. And, just as the Samaritan woman that met Jesus boldly told everyone about Him, your testimony to hurting or rejected people can change their lives and multiply God's love in your community.

delight |

How do social conventions and racism prevent people from knowing and following Jesus?

Why should we step beyond those borders to talk about Jesus?

Called

display |

Think of some ways you can turn your community into a mission field. Look for an area of your school or your community that your youth group or your family could go and share the love of Jesus. Consider planting flowers at an apartment complex or providing food to someone who is hungry. Look for ways to serve those who typically provide a service to you. Write an idea below of how you can tangibly show the love of God like Jesus did to the Samaritan woman.

God, thank You for stepping over boundaries to make believers. Everyone has the right to know You, and I pray that You would help me let go of any bias I may have so that I can speak to others and share my faith. I pray for boldness to change hearts and communities. Amen.

REDEEMED

discover |

READ LUKE 8:1-3; JOHN 20:11-18.

*Jesus said to her, "Mary." Turning around, she said to him in
Aramaic, "Rabboni!"—which means "Teacher." —John 20:16*

One of the amazing things about Jesus's earthly ministry was His
compassion for those who were hurting and rejected. Jesus met them
in their place of pain, restored them, and created a forever relationship
with them. Remember the man cutting himself in the graveyard (see
Mark 5:5), the woman at the well (see John 4), or the man with the
withered hand (see Mark 3)? Each time, there was a touch from Jesus
that took their lives in a new direction. Jesus redeemed them and
restored them.

Mary Magdalene had seven demons that were tormenting her and
destroying her life. Jesus saved her from that terrible condition. Today,
you or someone you know is probably enduring terrible circumstances
that challenges their ability to function—things like depression, divorce,
abuse, and other terrible circumstances that haunt lives. Jesus looks
beyond what people have been through and are currently going
through. He rebuilds and reminds us that His death on the cross
changes everything. Today's circumstances are not the end of the story.
Jesus sees and redeems.

The best part is that when we have a genuine connection with Jesus,
we learn that He never lets us go. At the empty tomb, Jesus called
Mary by her name and not her past. He intentionally seeks us out and
will continually call us to follow Him and share His story. Mary was the
first person at the tomb and the first to tell the story of Jesus's return.

delight |

What do you think it means to be redeemed?

How can you share with someone that Jesus knows about their pain and still pursues them?

display |

Redeem means something is gained in exchange for something. Jesus gave His life in exchange for ours even though it was an imperfect exchange. Think about how Jesus is okay with an unfair trade for love. Below, write out a word, sentence, or paragraph that describes your past. Then, cross it out and write the word "Redeemed" over it, around it, through it—any way you choose to symbolize that Jesus has power over your past.

Thank You, Jesus, that trophies are not reserved for those with the best beginning. Jesus, You can redeem us, and we can forever run to You despite where we have been. Help me today to see the hope You have for everyone amid their hurting. Amen.

BRING DOWN THE WALLS

discover |

READ LUKE 19:1-10.

"Today salvation has come to this house," Jesus told him, "because he too is a son of Abraham. For the Son of Man has come to seek and to save the lost." —Luke 19:9-10

In Arabic, Jericho means the city of the moon. Jericho is also the city where the walls crumbled when Joshua and the Israelites marched around them. The moon glows at night because it reflects the sun, and Jericho had walls to protect it from intruders. Teenagers can have a difficult time reflecting on a relationship with the Son of God because of the walls they have put up to mask things in their lives and prevent Jesus from getting to their hearts.

In today's passage, Jesus was passing through Jericho and met a short man standing in the branches of a tree. Jesus has a way of reaching people who feel too far away to be followers. Zacchaeus climbed a tree to see Jesus. Zacchaeus's profession as a tax collector gave him power and a terrible reputation. I believe Zacchaeus was running ahead of his reputation and climbing above his profession to see Jesus in a personal way.

Some teens base their entire identity on being the bad person and platform themselves above others because of that label. Jesus called Zacchaeus to come down from the tree quickly and asked to dine with Zacchaeus in his home. He knew what the crowd thought of Zacchaeus, but was more concerned about repentance and restoring Zacchaeus's reflection. That moment at the tree took down Zacchaeus's walls and allowed Jesus to enter his heart and home. The call from Jesus to a flawed Zacchaeus was to come down, repent, and follow.

delight |

What are ways people can separate from their reputation and fully live in their identity as a disciple of Jesus?

How do you think Zaccheus felt to be noticed for something good despite all the bad things everyone else had to say about him?

display |

Know in your heart today that sometimes when things feel like they are falling apart, they are actually falling into place. Jesus cares more about our repentance than our reputation. In order to follow Him wholeheartedly, we have to let our walls crumble and reflect who Jesus is. Today, when you get a chance, look past someone's reputation, position, or influence and love them the way Jesus does. Write out three ways you can love others in spite of their pasts below.

Thank You, Jesus, for seeing beyond reputations and offering us the chance for repentance. Help me to look for the heart of everyone and not what people say about them. Remind me that repentance can change hearts, remove walls, and revise reflections to mirror You. Amen.

TOUCHDOWN!

discover |

READ JOHN 12:1-8.

Then Mary took a pound of perfume, pure and expensive nard, anointed Jesus's feet, and wiped his feet with her hair. So the house was filled with the fragrance of the perfume. —John 12:3

I love American football. There are so many exciting elements to the game, but the best part is when a team scores a touchdown. There are multiple ways to score points, but only three ways to move the ball: run it, throw it, or kick it.

Some teams have to get creative and find different strategies using the methods available to find success moving the ball. Sometimes that means misdirection, trick plays, or doing things that surprise the defense. Regardless, the goal is always to score a touchdown.

Here is the point: God is calling all of us to love Him wholeheartedly, follow Him, and make disciples. Our forever goal is to love God and grow His kingdom. Martha followed Him with acts of service. Mary worshiped Him by anointing Him with perfume. Lazarus ate and reclined at the table with Him. There are seasons in discipleship to serve, to worship, and to fellowship with Christ. Just like how football teams have to get creative with how they move the ball, how we go about obtaining the goal of loving and growing God's kingdom differs. As you mature in knowing Jesus, you will grow in how you love and follow Him and lead others to Him.

delight |

What are some different ways we can worship God?

How has the way you show God you love Him changed since you first became a follower of Christ?

display

How you worship God is as unique as your fingerprint. Consider how you worship God, serve God, and tell others about Him. Take a moment today and have a unique worship time with Him. That could mean sitting in silence for a few minutes meditating on Him and His Word. It could be singing out loud to your favorite worship song. It could mean creating a piece of art that reflects what's happening in your heart as your worship. However you show your love for God today, see to it that it's genuine and from the heart.

God, I love the way You have given us seasons in life. Thank You for showing me multiple ways to worship and follow You. I pray now that I continue to grow through my seasons of serving You and following Your calling on my life. Amen.

HOW

HE

TAUGHT

THEM

What sets Jesus apart? What makes His call to discipleship any different from any other teacher ever? This section deals with this very idea. What Jesus taught His disciples and how He taught them turned the world upside down. He wasn't like anyone else, and He calls His followers to live in a way that is different from everyone else ever.

SOMETHING NEW

discover |

READ MATTHEW 5:43-48.

"You have heard that it was said, Love your neighbor and hate your enemy. But I tell you, love your enemies and pray for those who persecute you . . . " —Matthew 5:43–44

Excellence is an attitude, and perfection is a daily pursuit. While delivering His Sermon on the Mount, Jesus detailed a road map providing direction for His followers. In the final verses of Matthew 5, He shared the law of love and then provided the spirit behind it. His explanation of loving those we would rather despise was a serious challenge to His disciples then and to us now.

In fact, it was probably something His audience then would have never considered doing. What about you? When was the last time you did something you had never considered before?

When we are challenged to do something new, it charges us to grow and causes us to consider things we would usually ignore. Loving our enemies certainly is a challenge, but it does not mean we let our enemies mistreat us. Loving our enemies frees us from holding onto things that are only doing us damage. God's love tells us to stop and see things not from our perspectives, but from God's perspective. Jesus teaches us to trust Him over our feelings. Loving our enemies changes us before it changes them, but it requires daily determination to try. Love says, "I respect your opinion, I respect that you are God's creation, and I will give you respect." It is amazing what happens when we try something we had never considered, like that loving God means loving others—even our enemies. Following Jesus means doing things we would not do on our own.

Why are people hesitant to love their enemies?

What happens when we hold on to grudges?

Why does loving our enemies change us before it affects them?

Called

display |

Consider someone that you are holding a grudge against or are in a disagreement with. Write down below what your issue is with them, pray about it, then ask God to show you how to love them and see their side of the disagreement. This is what Jesus commanded us to do.

God, I thank You for challenging me to grow and do things outside of my comfort zone. As I journey to be a better follower of You, Jesus, help me see everyone through Your eyes, love others, and be open to doing something new—even loving my neighbor. Amen.

OWN THE POND

discover |

READ MATTHEW 6:5-15.

"But when you pray, go into your private room, shut your door, and pray to your Father who is in secret. And your Father who sees in secret will reward you." —Matthew 6:6

There is an old saying that goes, "Give a man a fish and he will eat for a day; teach a man to fish, and he will eat for the rest of his life." I like to add a third part to that saying. Not only should the man be taught how to fish, but how to own the pond.

The Lord's Prayer is taught to children and recited from adolescence into adulthood. You hear it at bedtime. It's prayed in locker rooms and recited at weddings. Yet, Jesus didn't give the disciples and us this prayer as a poem to memorize. Jesus was giving spiritual survival tips to own the pond.

The way Jesus taught was to tell truths that required action to obtain the promise. Jesus said, "when you pray." Prayer is a command, not a suggestion. Then He explained where and how to pray. After that, Jesus gave the promise that comes with prayer. My favorite part is where He said, in my own words, "God sees everything. God knows your needs and sees your story." When you open your mouth to talk to God, it allows you to admit you need Him. Friend, please note that the reward of your prayer is not more presents; it's God's presence. To possess God's promises and "own the pond," make prayer a discipline in your life and not an option.

delight |

How can you organize your day to prioritize prayer?

Why do you think Jesus encouraged the disciples to pray in private?

display |

If you are challenged to pray consistently, make a reminder on your phone that prompts you to pray every morning at a specific time. If you don't have a phone, put a note in a place where you will see it and be reminded everyday to pray. Scout out a quiet place for your prayer time and journal your thoughts. You can even use the note section on your phone, just avoid getting on social media during that time. Or you can use good old paper and pen. This prayer moment is only about you and God. Below, write out when you will take time out of your day to spend some private time in prayer.

Father God, thank You for always seeing me, even when I am not looking for You. Help me find a quiet place to pursue You and make prayer a discipline, not an option. Amen.

OBEDIENCE AND SACRIFICE

discover |

READ LUKE 9:12-17.

"You give them something to eat," he told them. "We have no more than five loaves and two fish," they said, "unless we go and buy food for all these people." (For about five thousand men were there.) Then he told his disciples, "Have them sit down in groups of about fifty each." —Luke 9:13–14

One of the most significant parts of following Christ is being invited into His miracles. Christ never asks us to explain how He makes miracles happen, but He does ask for us to be willing participants. In today's passage, the disciples were in a predicament. There were lots of hungry people, and the only readily accessible food was seemingly insufficient. A young boy appeared carrying two fish and five barley loaves. These fish and loaves were small portions for these hungry people. They needed a miracle.

Jesus can use anything to teach a lesson, and on that day, He had more than enough to make a miracle while teaching two main points—sacrifice and obedience. Obedience is done in love and sacrifice is uncomfortable. I don't know if the boy offered his lunch or it was requested from him. We know that it was all he had; to give it away was a sacrifice. Can you imagine the internal dialogue of the disciples as they prepared to provide Jesus with scraps to feed so many people? Love is shown through obedience. The disciples loved Jesus enough to trust that their little was enough. Obedience requires sacrifice, and the reward of both is worth more than what was given. Instead of trying to make it work in your head, be obedient, sacrifice your way, and let Christ work it out with His hands.

What does sacrifice look like to you?

Why do you think Jesus invites us to be a part of things that He could do on His own?

display |

Consider something you have held back because you felt it couldn't help. Knowing that sacrifice is uncomfortable and obedience is necessary, ask God about what you can give, and then do it in obedience. It may be uncomfortable, but remember that He honors your sacrifice and rewards your obedience. Is there is a miracle that is waiting on your sacrifice?

God, I thank You for choosing me to help make miracles happen. Forgive me for withholding what I felt was insufficient. Help me to recognize that sacrifice is effort while remaining enthusiastic about the rewards of obedience. Amen.

THIRSTY

discover |

READ JOHN 6:22-40.

"I am the bread of life," Jesus told them. "No one who comes to me will ever be
hungry, and no one who believes in me will ever be thirsty again." —John 6:35

In the 8th grade, I attended a youth conference that featured a team of
bodybuilders using their physical strength to share the gospel. When
the bodybuilders gave the invitation to know Christ, I came running. I
believed getting saved would make me physically strong like them. At
home, I read the Scriptures they shared and waited for my muscles to
start growing. Nothing happened physically, but spiritually I started
growing tremendously.

After feeding a multitude of people, Jesus gained followers, but they
were just chasing miracles (like I was chasing muscles). When the
crowds found Jesus, He turned their hunger into a lesson on life. Jesus
wanted them to see that the miracle was more than a giant helping of
food. A relationship with God would help them have eternal life.

"Thirsty" is an urban phrase for overly desiring attention. Too often,
when people are "thirsty," they will take anything to satisfy their craving
for attention. Jesus said the same thing to the woman at the well, to
the people chasing miracles, and the same thing to you—believing in
Jesus will quench your thirst. Not your craving for attention, but the
fulfillment for the hole in your soul that can only be filled by Him. Stay
hungry for Jesus more than anything else, and He will satisfy your thirst.

delight |

Why do you think the people chased miracles over wanting a relationship with Jesus?

How can we find our hunger and thirst fulfilled in Jesus rather than in our desires?

display |

Take a moment to consider your prayer life. When you pray, seek to know God, and ask that He satisfy you more than anything else. Write out a prayer below and ask Him to fulfill your every need and lead you to righteousness.

Dear God, I thank You for every miraculous thing You have made occur in my life. Yet, I pray now that I seek You more than the stuff I want. Help me to quench my thirst through You as I remain hungry for a more significant relationship with You. Amen.

ORIENTATION

discover |

READ LUKE 9:1-6.

Summoning the Twelve, he gave them power and authority over all the demons and to heal diseases. Then he sent them to proclaim the kingdom of God and to heal the sick. —Luke 9:1-2

Getting your first job is a badge of honor. It means that you have graduated into the next stage of growing up and can begin to earn the resources to help provide for yourself. My first job was at a grocery store. At work, I represented the company and was part of growing the store. You don't know everything before your first day at work, and that's okay. The company manager will have an orientation to teach you how to be successful.

When Jesus called His disciples, He equipped them. That means He trained them, kind of like the company orientation. Orientation gives direction. When we sit with Jesus as His disciples, He provides directions before He sends us to work. Jesus could do great miracles; however, His equipped team of disciples was an extension of Himself and helped extend the growth of God's kingdom. Jesus told the disciples that they had everything they needed and launched them out to participate in kingdom work. He also told them to move on when their presence was not received.

You are also a part of Team Jesus, and your orientation class is here through growing as a disciple. You have the opportunity to participate in the work of Christ by telling everyone about Him.

delight |

What direction is Jesus sending you to work?

How does it feel that the company president (Jesus) wants you to work for Him?

display

Seek God about your direction. Ask Him about the best ways to serve as a staff member on Team Jesus. Then, as a staff member of God's kingdom, consider your actions as you represent Christ. Write out below three ways you can serve on Team Jesus today.

 1.

 2.

 3.

God, I thank You for choosing me to participate in Your work. Help me hear the direction You want me to go and be mindful of places where I need to leave. Amen.

BRUISES OR TATTOOS?

discover |

READ MATTHEW 17:14-20.

"Lord," he said, "have mercy on my son, because he has seizures and suffers terribly. He often falls into the fire and often into the water. I brought him to your disciples, but they couldn't heal him." —Matthew 17:15-16

Have you ever fallen and gotten a bruise? What happens in a few days? It goes away. On the flip side, have you ever gotten a tatoo? If you have and you don't like the result, it is no small task to get rid of it. The internet is littered with "tattoo fails." It's easy to fall into the trap of believing that failure is proof we aren't good enough or not supposed to be where God has sent us. That could not be further from the truth.

In today's passage, a father went to the disciples to heal his son, but they couldn't do it. He then turned to Jesus to see if He could help. It's like when a younger sibling asks an older sibling to help them with their problems and then asks a parent to fix what the older sibling could not. Jesus taught the disciples then sent them out. Somehow, while doing what they were told to do, they were unsuccessful. It hurts when we don't achieve what we set out to accomplish. That doesn't mean we should quit our overall plan. We just need to reevaluate how we are going about it. We have to check our motives and our hearts.

Jesus took this moment of failure to educate the disciples instead of expelling them from teaching and healing. Jesus took their failure and talked them through why their ministry had to be more than going through the motions, bigger than saying the right words, and greater than just being on team Jesus. Failure can be good when we learn from it. Remember, failures are bruises and not tattoos.

delight |

What is something you have failed at that is worth trying again?

Why do you think God lets us fail at times?

display |

Step back from the place or circumstance where you did not get it right.
Evaluate your motives, learn from your mistakes, then give yourself a break.
Jesus gave the disciples a second chance. Don't you think you deserve one also?
In the space below, write out a prayer asking God to help you try again in an
area where you have failed. Ask Him to reveal your motives, to give you the right
motives, and to help you have the right heart.

God, thank You for allowing me to try. Help me to see that my mistakes
are bruises and not tattoos. Show me when my motive is mistaken and
my action is incorrect. I can learn from every failure. Help me see the
lesson in everything. Amen.

You call me Teacher and Lord—and you are speaking rightly, since that is what I am. So if I, your Lord and Teacher, have washed your feet, you also ought to wash one another's feet. For I have given you an example, that you also should do just as I have done for you.

CHILDLIKE FAITH

discover |

READ LUKE 18:15-17.

Jesus, however, invited them: "Let the little children come to me, and don't stop them, because the kingdom of God belongs to such as these." —Luke 18:16

Life is to be enjoyed, and loving God should be a fun experience. Sometimes, for some people, things change when they get locked into doing life and stop enjoying it. In today's Scripture, a group of parents was attempting to bring their children to Jesus for Him to bless them. Before the kids could get too close, the disciples stopped the children and fussed at the parents.

A significant barrier to being close to God is getting caught up in our plans. Jesus is for everyone and especially appreciates when we have a pure heart and open relationship with Him. Childlike faith says, "Jesus, I trust You and want to be near You." You can be serious and focused on your life and still love Jesus with joy and unbridled affection. Think about how you feel when you are in the presence of someone you admire. Daily, we should feel excited, encouraged, and inspired when we consider that Jesus is always with us.

Our lives are often the only Bible that someone will read. It does Jesus and the kingdom of God a great disservice if we are turning people away from the one who is calling everyone by how we represent Christ. Jesus called the children to Him despite what the disciples said and used this moment to teach the disciples the importance of childlike faith.

delight |

How do you maintain childlike excitement about Jesus?

What can you do to make sure you don't suffocate someone else's childlike faith?

Called

display |

Review how you see your relationship with Jesus. Have you allowed life or others to stop you from having childlike faith? Spend time removing those barriers and rekindle your childlike faith again. Have fun in God's presence, trust God without question, and read His Word to see how much He loves you. Below, write one barrier to childlike faith that you have. Beneath it, write one way to overcome that barrier and restore childlike faith in your life.

God, You desire childlike faith. I pray that any barriers to my faith in You would be removed so that I can revel in your presence and rejoice in Your blessings. Help me not to block others from having childlike faith in You as well. Amen.

KEEP WALKING

discover |

READ MATTHEW 14:22-33.

Immediately Jesus spoke to them. "Have courage! It is I. Don't be afraid."
"Lord, if it's you," Peter answered him, "command me to come to you on the water."
He said, "Come." —Matthew 14:27-29

Peter and the disciples were in a storm without Jesus physically in their boat. At 3 a.m., the storm was shaking their faith, but suddenly their seemingly absent Savior appeared, walking on water. I don't know if curiosity or blind optimism made Peter ask Jesus if he could join Him on the water, but I do know that Jesus used this miraculous moment to teach a valuable lesson about trust. How can someone whipped by wind and blinded by rain see Jesus? How can that same person even muster the courage to step out of the boat? Trust. Peter had enough trust to step onto the water but lacked the continuous trust to complete the journey to Jesus.

We often find that our ability to trust can shift like Peter's. The rain kept falling and the wind continued blowing while Peter was walking toward Jesus, but Jesus remained right in front of Peter the entire time. The same is true for us. We must develop an unshakable trust to step out of the boat and to keep walking, even when it's difficult.

Trusting Jesus doesn't stop storms, but trusting in Jesus prevents storms from stopping us. Boats don't sink because of the water around them. They sink when the water gets inside of them. When Peter's focus shifted from Jesus to the storm, He began to sink. Just as Peter fell, though, he felt the firm grip of Jesus yanking him back to his feet. Jesus earned the trust of the disciple. You can trust Jesus in blinding storms and in the sinking situations, too.

delight |

What everyday activity can feel like a storm in your life?

Does it take more trust to get out of the boat or to walk on water? Why?

display |

The physical Jesus is more than in front of you—He is inside of you through the Holy Spirit. Trust what is on the inside. Trust when Jesus encourages your next big steps, then keep Jesus in front of you and trust Him every step of the way. Get creative in the space below. Write a poem or draw a picture that symbolizes the faith you want to have in Jesus. He is there. He loves you. You can trust Him!

Dear God, thank You for encouraging my giant leaps in life. Even in the darkest hours and through blinding storms, help me always see You and trust You to make miracles happen. Forgive me for seeing more in the storm than I see in You. I know that I can walk through difficult times with You and I can stand strong in uncertain spaces. Amen.

Called

THE LITTLE THINGS

discover |

READ JOHN 13:1-17.

"You call me Teacher and Lord—and you are speaking rightly, since that is what I am. So if I, your Lord and Teacher, have washed your feet, you also ought to wash one another's feet. For I have given you an example, that you also should do just as I have done for you." —John 13:13–15

For three years, Jesus taught, healed, and did the miraculous with His close crew of companions. The disciples followed Jesus with great enthusiasm and commitment to His teaching. In His last days on earth, Jesus took the disciples to an upstairs room for a special meal and a request. This final meal, shared by all of the disciples, occurred before Jesus was tried and subsequently crucified.

Here is where the story gets good. Before the dinner, Jesus removed His robe, wrapped a towel around His waist, poured water into a basin, and began washing the disciples' feet. It was the ultimate sign of humility. People didn't wear closed-toe tennis shoes back then. Everyone walked in sandals and attracted dust, dung, and all types of dirt as they traveled. Jesus washing their feet meant He was personally addressing whatever nasty stuff they were carrying on the dirtiest part of their bodies. Jesus didn't mind getting His hands dirty for His friends.

As Jesus tied His towel around His waist and made His basin of water, He was further exhibiting the service He would expect from His disciples. Removing His robe and washing their feet was ultimately about humble service. Jesus will never ask us to do more for others than He has already done for us. Jesus led by example, taught through examples, and asks His disciples to be an example. Never be too big to do the little things for others that Jesus has done for you.

delight |

What stops you from wanting to do the dirty work for Jesus?

Why is it essential for leaders to also be servants?

display |

Take off pride this week and find a way to serve someone who typically takes care of you. Consider showing appreciation to your parents in a unique way, helping your siblings, or doing an act of service for a close friend. Afterwards, review this Scripture with them and let them know Jesus washing His disciples' feet was your motivation for service. Ask them how they could do the same for others also.

Thank You, God, for sending Jesus, a living example for how we should live. Help me remain humble as I serve others. Help me recognize moments when people I follow are humble toward me. Remind me that I should never consider myself too big to serve others. Amen.

F-R-I-E-N-D-S

discover |

READ JOHN 15:9-17.

"I do not call you servants anymore, because a servant doesn't know what his master is doing. I have called you friends, because I have made known to you everything I have heard from my Father." —John 15:15

Friends carry a significant place of honor in our lives. There is a saying that goes "Friends are the family we choose for ourselves." Did you know that Jesus specifically, intentionally, and purposefully chose you? Our Scripture for today reveals that Jesus didn't just want followers, He wanted friends as well.

Your friendship is significant. When we look at today's passage, we get another glance at how Jesus cared for His disciples. Although Jesus was the clear leader and held the position of authority, He did not position Himself so far above His disciples that He could not know them personally.

Jesus taught about friendship and proved His true friendship by laying down His life. When we lay something down, that means we release it, let it go, or diminish its prominence. Jesus told the disciples that He loved them the way God loves Him. God gave His only Son, and Jesus gave His life.

Jesus teaches us to hang out in that space called His love and experience a joy that fills and overflows. The reason your joy overflows is because Jesus wants anyone near you to experience the runoff of what He has given you. Happiness comes and goes. Endless joy is from committed friendship with Jesus Christ.

delight |

How do you think the disciples felt when Jesus, the Son of God, called them His friends?

What is a way that we can lay down our lives for our friends?

display

Jesus laid down His life for friendship. If letting go is a way of letting someone know you love them, consider letting go of popularity to prove your friendship, releasing time to tell someone you are there for them, or serving in a way that doesn't give you credit. Do everything in love, not for love. Below, write down three ways you can show your friends that you love them.

God, thank You for loving me and reminding me to stay in Your love. I pray that I am careful to consider others and consciously lay down my life for my friends. Amen.

WHAT HE CALLED THEM TO

Following Jesus is not always easy, but it's always right. Jesus called His followers then and today to be fully devoted to Him, to walk with Him in faithfulness, and to live in a way that reveals the truth of who He is. This final section of the book will help give you a handle on some of the most important elements of what Jesus calls His followers to, who He calls us to be, and what He wants to do in our lives.

HEAVY CROSS

discover |

READ MATTHEW 16:24-28.

Then Jesus said to his disciples, "If anyone wants to follow after me, let him deny himself, take up his cross, and follow me. For whoever wants to save his life will lose it, but whoever loses his life because of me will find it." —Matthew 16:24-25

An empty water bottle doesn't weigh very much. But if you were to put that regular 16-ounce water bottle in your hand, then extend your arm straight out in front of you, over time, that empty bottle will become unbearable. The same thing is true when we live selfishly. Initially, doing things our way is fun and easy, but it becomes painfully difficult the longer we do it.

Jesus clearly explained what it takes to be His follower. He said you must deny yourself, take up your cross, and follow Him. He tells us to stop belly-button gazing and fix our focus on Him. The conversation we read today in Scripture occurred within a chapter where Jesus predicted His death—and not long before He was crucified. He was calling the disciples, then and now, to do some heavy lifting.

Living a selfish life is ultimately hard and hurtful; however, carrying our cross comes with help and lengthens our life eternally. No one knows the exact weight of the cross Jesus carried, but we know it wasn't the beautiful sculpture hanging in our churches or the sterling silver medallion hanging from our necklace. The cross was a rough, jagged, and uncomfortable object, and so is our calling to love others. We can either sit down and sulk or stand up, carry this thing, and follow Christ. Jesus taught the disciples to take up their crosses and follow Him because He would show them how to handle the weight of a cross properly and what it means.

delight |

What does your cross look like?

Why did Jesus tell the disciples to let go of their lives before picking up the cross?

display |

Crosses are heavy but manageable. It is not the weight, but how you carry it. Talk to God about your life, read how He handled circumstances in the Bible, and follow His actions in your life. In the cross drawing below, write around it the things you need to get rid of. Then, on the inside of it, write the things you need to pick up and do.

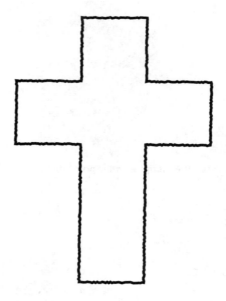

God, my cross is heavy, but I thank You for being the ultimate example of handling it. I release my way so that I can do Your will. Help me to follow Your lead in every area of my life. Amen.

"ARE YOU ABOUT THIS LIFE?"

discover |

READ LUKE 14:25-33.

*"If anyone comes to me and does not hate his own father and
mother, wife and children, brothers and sisters—yes, and even
his own life—he cannot be my disciple." —Luke 14:26*

One day I was working out with my younger, yet stronger brother. The
beginning of the workout was great. Right when I thought we were
wrapping up, my brother stacked the bar with bigger weights. He
showed me how to bench the weight, then said, "Are you about this
life?" It was time to make a decision to get serious about working out
or go home.

In Luke 14, while traveling with the disciples and a large group of
people, Jesus turned to the crowd and made a challenging statement:
"Love me above everybody and everything else." Yep, even your family.
He didn't want them to hate their family—God created family.

Jesus was challenging their intentions and priorities. He wanted the
crowd to consider if they were chasing miracles or following Him. Jesus
taught that tough choices are necessary, consideration is needed, and
He must never come second. There isn't an easy way to do something
difficult, but choosing to love Christ over everything else in life is always
the right decision.

delight |

Why do you think Jesus was adamant about His position in the lives of the crowd and the disciples?

How can we keep Christ at the forefront of what we love?

display |

Shift Jesus to the forefront of what you love. What we love is proven by where we spend our time. Give God the first few moments of every morning and watch how He returns that love and how you'll grow. In the space below, write out things that are in your life, family, school work, sports, video games, etc. Then, next to each item, list out how you can love Jesus first in those things. You don't have to quit your life to follow Jesus. He just wants everything about your life to reveal that He is number one.

Jesus, You taught me to love You above anything else. Help me to recognize when my priorities are shifting from You, and my decisions are too quick. I want the life You prepared for me, and I want to give up everything that would hinder me from having it. Amen.

Called

TIME TO SHINE

discover |

READ MATTHEW 5:14-16.

"In the same way, let your light shine before others, so that they may see your good works and give glory to your Father in heaven." —Matthew 5:16

You are a one-of-a-kind creation and there will never be another you. When God created you, He was so impressed that He broke the mold. Whether you know it or not, inside you—through the Holy Spirit—is a light that shines so brightly, everyone wants to see it. But, like any brilliant light, what makes you unique is how you shine and what you light up.

Jesus shared with His disciples that they were providing light to dark areas through their presence. But their light should direct others to what makes them shine. Jesus is the light of the world (see John 1:5), and we are the reflection.

You might ask, "How can I shine?" Consider the times athletes point to the sky after they score or when celebrities thank God first in their acceptance speeches. You can shine through your ability to paint amazingly, sing beautifully, dance wonderfully, play sports authoritatively, or excel academically, among other activities and things. When you use the gifts and talents that God gave you for His glory, these fantastic moments are your time to remind yourself and others that it is only through Christ that you can do all things!

delight |

Why should God get the glory for accomplishments and attention you receive?

How can you shine and show people that God gave you the ability and deserves the glory?

display |

Make giving God credit a habit. Immediately following anything you excel at today, stop and thank God. "Praise God" is a statement and a declaration. If anyone celebrates you for something you have done well today, tell them God helped you achieve it. If they don't know about God, use that moment to talk about who God is to you.

Thank You, God, for choosing me to be a light. Thank You for every ability You have given me and every chance I get to shine. I pray that I always point people to You. I will give You glory for the rest of my life. Amen.

FACTS VS. TRUTH

discover |

READ JOHN 8:31-32.

"You will know the truth, and the truth will set you free." —John 8:32

There is a difference between facts and the truth. If we are not careful, we will allow facts to overshadow the truth and constrict us from living the full life Christ intends for us.

Laws are meant to provide borders and protect people. During the time of Jesus, certain religious leaders would take religious laws and overly enforce them. In today's verses, Jesus was talking to new believers. He acknowledged their beginning, then pressed them to continue believing. When you are persistent, you can get what you want. When you are consistent, you will maintain what you achieve. Jesus was teaching consistency in faith, not strict, oppressive observance of laws that weigh us down and divert us from the freedom of the gospel.

The freedom Jesus spoke about was liberty of thought and faith that only comes from more than quick visits with God. Jesus told the disciples to move in permanently and stay. When we move in and stay, facts don't overshadow truth. Facts say you don't have enough—truth says, my God shall supply all of your needs (see Phil. 4:19). Facts say you are fighting sickness—truth says, by the stripes of Jesus Christ, you are healed (see Isa. 53:5). Facts say friends leave when you need them most—truth says God sticks closer than a brother (see Prov. 18:24) and promises never to leave you or forsake you (Heb. 13:5). Recognize facts, but rest in the truth that gives you the liberty to live in the freedom God has called you to.

Called

delight |

What truth can you find to combat facts in your life?

What is an example of freedom achieved from moving into a permanent relationship with God?

display |

Jesus taught that when we abide in His presence, we will find freedom. Consider something you have been pondering so much that it has paused your life. Pray about it. But when you pray, don't run through your time like a track star. Hang out with God, stretch your quiet time beyond a few minutes and allow God to free your thoughts and give liberty to your actions.

Thank You, Jesus, for freedom. Thank You for teaching me to sit down in Your presence instead of speeding through my time with You. I pray that whatever is holding my thoughts and preventing me from living a free life in You be removed in the name of Jesus. Show me Your truth and help me see beyond roadblocks in my life. Amen.

Memory Verse
MATTHEW 11:28-30

"Come to me, all of you who are weary and burdened, and I will give you rest. Take up my yoke and learn from me, because I am lowly and humble in heart, and you will find rest for your souls. For my yoke is easy and my burden is light."

STAGE=STREETS

discover |

READ JOHN 13:31-35.

"I give you a new command: Love one another. Just as I have loved you, you are also to love one another. By this everyone will know that you are my disciples, if you love one another." —John 13:34-35

While attending a conference on youth ministry, I asked a teenager why she left the church. She said it was because the people on stage were not the same in the streets. The estimates of how many young people will leave the church in the next few years are staggering, but it doesn't have to be that way.

James Baldwin once said, "I don't believe what you say because I see what you do."[1] In other words, when our lives don't match our words, people don't believe what we say. Jesus taught His disciples to love their neighbors and instructed them to be a living example. The strongest argument for love comes from our actions, not from our words. Remember, you may be the only Bible someone reads today.

Jesus declared everyone would know His disciples followed Him because they loved one another. You have the ability to influence people all over the world by your love and respect for all people. The gospel is not reserved for one people group, and Jesus taught that our neighbors are more than those that look like us. Love is unlimited. Social media proves that you can know someone you have never met. Even if your followers don't like, share, subscribe, or retweet, it doesn't mean they didn't see it or weren't influenced by what you post. We can be recognized and be an influence from a distance.

delight |

Why are actions more influential than words?

How can we better monitor our actions?

What is a way you can better love your neighbor?

display |

Instead of being a Sunday stage model, be a role model every day. Let your stage self and your street self be the same. Choose Jesus, always. Don't win the argument but lose your witness. Seek someone outside of your circle to share God's love with—listen to their concerns, pray for them, help them with a school assignment, provide something they need, or just be friendly. If you have social media accounts, post a Scripture passage today and talk about how this reflects who you are trying to be and what God is doing in your life. If you don't use social media (and it's totally cool if you don't), then write a Scripture and put it in your car, on your bedroom door, bathroom mirror, or on the front of a school binder or folder. Display God's Word in a way where others will see it and interact with it.

Dear Jesus, You taught that people would know the disciples followed You because they loved others. Help me be a living example of Your love and help me to show love to others continuously. Jesus, I pray now that my everyday actions positively reflect a follower of You. Amen.

GRACE

discover |

READ JOHN 8:2-11.

When Jesus stood up, he said to her, "Woman, where
are they? Has no one condemned you?"
"No one, Lord," she answered.
"Neither do I condemn you," said Jesus. "Go, and from now
on do not sin anymore." —John 8:10–11

Remember when your mom or an authority figure saw you across the room and just sent that "I see you" stare instead of coming over? You didn't get away with anything. You were given a chance to get it right. Biblically, grace is something given freely by God despite our actions or attitude toward Him. No one is immune to getting in trouble, and everyone has the opportunity to get caught, but our response to grace is what matters.

In John 8, a woman was caught in a punishable act and brought to Jesus for a consequence. Jesus knew her accusers wanted an intense reaction but also wanted to see the demise of Jesus. Instead, Jesus gave them both grace. I wish I knew what Jesus wrote in the sand. Did He write the sins of her accusers? Did He write the names of those with the worst offenses? Or maybe He wrote down the definition of grace. She was caught in a punishable act, and they were caught up in their devious actions. But when He told them that the sinless ones could throw the first stones, the accusers walked away. The woman didn't have to explain her actions, and neither did the men wanting consequences. The just words of Jesus taught grace, changed hearts, and provided a path to righteousness. Jesus ended their short dialogue by saying, "Go, and . . . do not sin anymore."

delight |

How would you explain grace to a friend?

How do we make sure we are not taking advantage of grace?

display |

Consider when God has given you grace when you should have received something worse. Be grateful for grace and be aware of your actions. Extend grace to someone today and show them the path to knowing God.

God, I thank You for Your grace when I did not deserve it. Help me extend grace to others while being grateful for the grace You have given me. You have provided a path to righteousness through repentance. God, I admit where I have made mistakes and repent for my sins. I commit to making the right choices as I follow You. Amen.

Called

"THEY"

discover |

READ JOHN 6:60-69.

Simon Peter answered, "Lord, to whom will we go? You have the words of eternal life. We have come to believe and know that you are the Holy One of God." —John 6:68

Doing the right thing is still the right thing, even if the majority prefers the wrong thing. It sounds like a tongue twister, but "their" right is often wrong. A better question is who are "they"? "They" are usually a couple of people that we have mentally allowed to be the majority.

Our choices have eternal consequences, and choosing to follow Christ can be uncomfortable, but it's completely worth it. Remember, comfort and growth are enemies. As Jesus was teaching a group of disciples, He made comments that caused such discomfort that a majority chose to abandon following Him. Those disciples were more like fair-weather friends; only along for the good times. Jesus was challenging His disciples to be unapologetic believers that openly chose the words of Jesus over what "they" say (the world's ways).

Every criticism isn't a critique created to cut you down. The Bible is full of harsh statements that should challenge you and cause you to grow mentally, emotionally, and spiritually. When the majority of the disciples left, only the twelve remained. Simon Peter admitted that Jesus is the only source for life-giving instructions and professed Jesus's authority. Everyone has something to say, and opinions are common, but the Word of God is life-giving truth. "They" don't always know what is right, but the Lord does.

delight |

How do you stay faithful to what the Lord says is right when the majority says you are wrong?

How do we keep from becoming fair-weather followers of Jesus?

display |

Jesus desires a real relationship with you, and that requires honest communication. Read the Ten Commandments (see Ex. 20:1-17). If there is a difficult commandment for you to follow, talk to God about it, and ask Him to show you how to see it His way.

Jesus, I realize that following You may be offensive to others, but Your words are life to those who believe. I pray that even if the majority moves away from You, that You would provide me the strength to always stand for You. Help me to find growth when I am challenged. Amen.

LITTLE BIG LEADERS

discover |

READ MATTHEW 20:20-28.

"It must not be like that among you. On the contrary, whoever wants to become great among you must be your servant, and whoever wants to be first among you must be your slave . . . " —Matthew 20:26-27

The first four letters in minister and ministry spell the word "mini." In today's passage, Jesus taught about being the little big leader. Little big leaders hold the boss title but serve like new employees. In other words, they may be the CEO, but they aren't afraid to sweep the floor also. This is how Jesus called His disciples to be.

Friend, success is great and achievement is amazing, but when you get to heaven, you should value God's "well done" over having achieved positions of power. We live in a society where everyone is jockeying for position. Just notice, as soon as a new iPhone® drops, their competitors will put something out that is "better than the iPhone®." It's a dog-eat-dog world, and we are not called to get tangled up in it.

It's okay to push yourself to succeed, but serve well during your effort. Most of all, be well-known by God. After all, all promotions and any elevation we receive comes from Him. Ultimately, according to Jesus, great leaders are great servants. Remember, this is the man who washed the feet of His disciples. Being a well-known boss includes being a willing servant to everyone.

delight

When have you seen a boss be a servant, and how did it make you feel?

Why do you think Jesus puts such an emphasis on serving others?

display |

Take time today to serve your neighbor. If you are on varsity athletics, help mentor the freshman. If you are excelling academically, help tutor someone who is struggling with your best subject. If you are first chair in the band, take time to help out the student in the last chair. Wherever you are known as the leader, reach back to someone who is not on your leadership level without the expectation of applause.

Dear God, help me stay humble and love others as I seek to succeed. Thank You for reminding me that achieving number-one success means serving like someone without status. The promotion comes from You, and I pray that above all else, my actions are always pleasing to You. Amen.

SOMEONE WHO CAN SEE

discover |

READ LUKE 6:39-40.

He also told them a parable: "Can the blind guide the blind? Won't they both fall into a pit? A disciple is not above his teacher, but everyone who is fully trained will be like his teacher."

It is better to lead people to places we have been before. Why? Because we know the way. Jesus, while giving instructions about judging others, used an illustration about two blind individuals. Since neither could see, they would not be very good guides for one another. What this means is that in order to lead others, we must first be led by someone who can see clearly—Jesus.

God gave every person a passion for progress, knowing we would have some limitations. Although progress varies between individuals, we all need proper leadership to assist in our journey. What this means is that we don't have to be perfect to lead others toward Jesus. After all, Jesus found us in spite of our flaws.

As disciples of Jesus, if we're going to lead others to the light of Jesus, we need to know the light for ourselves. As leaders, we must hang out extensively with other leaders. As worshipers, we must spend personal time in worship. Jesus is the light; Therefore, to help others see the light, His disciples should seek to be like Him. Scripture says fully trained students will become like the teacher. In order to be like our teacher, Jesus, we can't stop growing. We must endeavor to learn as much as possible about where we are going and let God provide the instructions.

delight

How do we become fully trained?

What is the benefit of leading someone to a place where you have been before?

display |

Share a story with a friend about how knowing God led you out of a dark time in your life. Talk about Scriptures that are helpful for light in life's darkest moments. Write three verses down below that have been helpful to you in dark moments. Share them with your friend if the opportunity arises.

Thank You, God, for being a present help in a time of need. When I find myself in dark areas of life, remind me of Your words that promise to be a lamp to my feet and light to my path. Help me also to be a light that leads others to Your guiding and comforting light. Amen.

YOKED

discover |

READ MATTHEW 11:28-30.

"Come to me, all of you who are weary and burdened, and I will give you rest. Take up my yoke and learn from me, because I am lowly and humble in heart, and you will find rest for your souls. For my yoke is easy and my burden is light."

Life is less complicated than we often make it. With everything going on in our lives, we often overcomplicate and overanalyze things. However, Jesus says, "I have an app for that." Not really, but what I mean by that is Jesus says, "I have the answers." At the tip of our fingers, we have the ability to access answers instantly to everything we can imagine. But here's the thing—search engines may offer suggestions, but the answers they provide aren't always right.

Jesus told His disciples that He understood everything that concerned them and promised to help them carry the load. The weight of our thoughts and questions can cripple us mentally, but Jesus calls us to shift the weight onto Him and allow Him to help.

The rest Jesus offers is not relinquishing responsibility. Rather, it is shared strength. A yoke was a tool strapped across oxen that helped guide them and allowed them to pull huge loads of weight. A more experienced ox was strapped to a younger ox with a yoke to teach and train the younger one. Jesus called His disciples to come to Him, connect with Him, and rest in Him. He calls us to do the same. Let Jesus answer your questions, lead you, and teach you how to shoulder responsibility while stepping forward in faith. There's no better person to be yoked with than Jesus.

delight |

What happens to you when you try to shoulder too much weight for too long all by yourself?

How do you give your cares to Jesus?

display |

Write down the heaviest stuff you are dealing with right now. After you compile your list, talk to God about each item and ask Him how to deal with your cares one by one. If you have a friend who seems weighed down by worry, walk them through this exercise, then pray with them about God's direction. Move forward patiently while pursuing God's peace and strength every step of the way.

Thank You, God, that You don't want us to shoulder our worries alone. The weight of anxiety is heavy, but that is not how You prefer that we live. I can do challenging things well because, with You, all things are possible. Because of You, I am never alone. I cast my cares on You and ask that You help me step forward in power with Your peace. Amen.

Marked by Love

Jesus called His disciples to live for Him, and in the last section of this devotional, we took a closer look at what that means. But every command Jesus gave about following Him can be summed up today just as He summed it up for people then: "Love the Lord your God with all your heart, with all your soul, with all your mind, and with all your strength. The second is, Love your neighbor as yourself. There is no other command greater than these" (Mark 12:30-31). Our lives are to be marked by love, for God above all and for others.

We aren't meant to live isolated lives, but to live in relationship with God and others. Starting with your closest relationships and then working outward, come up with at least one way you can show love to each of these people groups.

If it helps, you can picture your relationships like this (the smallest circle being the closest in relationship to you to you):

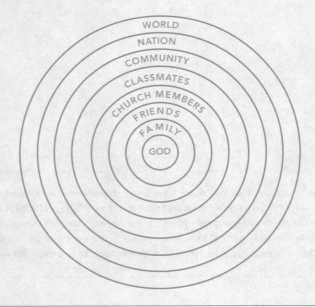

If you get stuck, consider using these questions:

- How can I show my love to God? How can I live so others see my love for God?

- How can I show love to my family? How can I live so others see my love for my family?

- How can I show love to my friends?

- What are some ways I can show love to the members of my youth group or church?

- How can I show my classmates that I love them?

- Thinking specifically about the needs of my local community, what are some things I can do to show love to my neighbors?

- How can I show love to people across the nation, whether I know them or not? (Hint: Think of ministries your church might be involved in or that your parents support.)

- In what ways can I show love to the world at large? What specific things can I do to show love to the oppressed and disenfranchised?*

*As always, before you act on any of these things, it's a good idea to seek guidance from a parent or guardian and your pastor or youth pastor. See where your family and church are already involved.

Ultimately, it all boils down to one simple question: What will you do to live a life marked by the love of Jesus?

PLANTED

Jesus spent a lot of time teaching people—not for His own benefit or so He could gain more followers, but so He could lead people to the Father and to living the abundant and full life He promised (see John 10:10). He pointed consistently to the truth that an abundant life starts by abiding with God—and He used plant imagery to teach this, calling Himself the Vine, God the Gardener, and us the branches (see John 15:1-17). This would've been a familiar idea to God's people, as Israel had also been called a vineyard or vine throughout the Old Testament (see Ps. 1:1-3; 80; Isa. 5:1-7). This wasn't the only plant imagery used— Jesus also frequently talked about producing fruit when teaching His disciples how to live godly lives. Take a look:

"You did not choose me, but I chose you. I appointed you to go and produce fruit and that your fruit should remain, so that whatever you ask the Father in my name, he will give you." —John 15:16

Now, that might be an odd sounding phrase to us today, no matter how many times we've heard it in church or Bible studies or devotional books like this one. Essentially, Jesus was saying the fruit people produce is "the qualities manifested in their lives"[2]—just as the fruit of the Spirit comes from the Holy Spirit's work in our lives (see Gal. 5:22-23).

We've already looked at one fruit Jesus's followers should produce: love. But aside from that, throughout the Gospels to the end of the New Testament, believers in Jesus are called to do many things as we follow Him that point others to the Father. Simply put, we are to produce fruit.

In each piece of fruit/tree branch on this page—and using Scripture as your guide—write out the different ways Jesus teaches people to produce fruit. Then prayerfully commit to doing these things in your own life.

Called

NOTES

1. James Baldwin, "A Report from Occupied Territory," *The Nation*, July 11, 1966, https://www.thenation.com/article/archive/report-occupied-territory/.

2. Trent C. Butler et al., eds., *Holman Illustrated Bible Dictionary* (Nashville, TN: Holman Reference, 2003), 603.